Secrets of Sound

Secrets of Sound

Studying the Calls and Songs of Whales, Elephants, and Birds

by **April Pulley Sayre**

Houghton Mifflin Company   Boston 2002

For my mother, Elizabeth Richardson Pulley, a great listener
—A. P. S.

Acknowledgments

I am deeply grateful to the following people who made this book possible by giving generously of their time and expertise: Katy Payne, Mya Thompson, and Melissa Groo at the Elephant Listening Project of the Cornell Lab of Ornithology's Bioacoustics Research Program; Bill Evans of Old Bird; Dr. Jan Randall of San Francisco State University; Dr. Ron Hoy of the Cornell University Department of Neurology and Behavior; Dr. Sandra Gaunt of the Ohio State University Borror Laboratory of Bioacoustics; Dr. Bill Barklow of Framingham State College; Dr. Christopher Clark of the Cornell Laboratory of Ornithology's Bioacoustics Research Program; and wildlife photographer Lynda Richardson.

Photo on page 1 by April Pulley Sayre. *Scientists listen in on underwater concerts sung by humpback whales.*
Photo on page 2 by Joyce Poole. *Katy Payne studies the sounds and behaviors of elephants.*
Photo on page 64 by Jeff Sayre. *Albatrosses open their bills and then snap them closed during a courtship display.*

www.houghtonmifflinbooks.com

Book design by Lisa Diercks
The text of this book is set in Minion.

Library of Congress Cataloging-in-Publication Data
Sayre, April Pulley.
Secrets of sound : studying the calls and songs of whales, elephants, and birds / by April Pulley Sayre.
p. cm.
Includes bibliographical references (p.).
Summary: Examines the work of several bioacousticians, scientists who study the sounds made by living creatures, discussing the results and importance of their research.
ISBN 0-618-01514-0
1. Bioacoustics—Juvenile literature. [1. Animal sounds.] I. Title.
QH510.5 .S28 2002   599.159—dc21   2001051877

Printed in Singapore
TWP 10 9 8 7 6 5 4 3 2 1

Contents

Hippos can talk to one another above and below water. PHOTO BY LYNDA RICHARDSON

Introduction

Squeaks. Wails. Whistles. Snorts. Songs. Drumming. All over the globe, animals are making sounds, and these days, more than *ever*, scientists are listening to them. In a desert in Uzbekistan, Dr. Jan Randall records sounds that wild gerbils make when they thump their feet on the ground. At a waterhole in Africa, Dr. Bill Barklow listens to the recently discovered underwater sounds of hippos. In Texas, Bill Evans rigs up microphones to record and identify the mysterious calls of night-migrating birds.

Meanwhile, on a ship off the coast of Hawaii, Christopher Clark lowers a special microphone into the ocean to listen to whales singing. He also analyzes secret recordings from hundreds of ocean microphones that the navy uses to track enemy submarines. The microphones record not just submarine noises but also, by accident, the songs of whales.

Scientists who study animal sounds are called bioacousticians, or acoustic biologists. Bioacoustics is the study of sounds made by living things. (Acoustics is the study of sound.) Bioacousticians study sounds made by mammals, insects, birds, frogs, and other creatures.

In recent years, hidden sounds—beyond the normal range of human hearing—have provided a whole new field of exploration. Katy Payne has discovered that elephants make sounds—low, loud, and deep—that travel for many miles. Some of these sounds are too low for humans to hear, but people can feel them as a throbbing in the air.

Bioacousticians come from a wide range of backgrounds. Some start from a love of science,

Bill Barklow, a bioacoustic pioneer, listens to the underwater sounds of hippos. PHOTO BY LYNDA RICHARDSON

others from a love of music or engineering. Over the years, many of these bioacousticians have worked together. Often what one bioacoustician discovers helps someone else. Their discoveries have built on one another, like notes in a symphony. Together, they are seeking a better understanding of the sounds animals make, what those sounds mean, and how to use this knowledge to help save endangered animals.

Christopher Clark and a colleague get a close-up look at a right whale off the coast of Argentina. PHOTO BY JANE MOON CLARK

Wondering About Whales

Christopher Clark

Christopher Clark grew up in a house full of music. When he was nine, he attended a special boarding school for choir singers at St. John the Divine in New York City. He was definitely "tuned in" to sound from an early age—but back then, he wasn't listening to whales.

Today, Dr. Clark uses underwater microphones, called hydrophones, to hear the songs of whales. He is researching how whales use sound to navigate, communicate, and survive in the ocean. Clark is director of the Bioacoustics Research Program at the Cornell Lab of Ornithology in Ithaca, New York. There he works in laboratories, with computers, to analyze the whale songs he records. He also coordinates the work of other scientists who study birds, elephants, and other animals.

Clark loves his work. "I have to admit, I have a great job," he says. "I wouldn't trade it for the world." His favorite part of the job is studying whales in the wild.

To record whale sounds, Clark lowers a hydrophone about thirty-five feet down into the ocean. Using a headset attached to the hydrophone, he can hear whales clearly. But even without hydrophones, the whale sounds can sometimes be heard by people sitting in the boats above. A boat's hull can vibrate and make strange noises as a

Top: *As a student, in 1974, Christopher Clark (in the hat) helped Roger Payne carry microphones to the whale recording site in Argentina.* PHOTO BY LYSA LELAND
Bottom: *Christopher Clark and the Paynes observed right whales from a hut on the coast of Argentina.* PHOTO BY CHRISTOPHER W. CLARK

whale sings. Centuries ago, sailors thought these sounds were made by mermaids.

Whales make many different kinds of sounds, from low rumbling noises to high squeaks. Beluga whales chirp, almost like birds. Male humpback whales sing songs that can last thirty minutes. Bowhead whales can imitate sounds such as ice cracking or the calls of beluga whales.

Clark began his career by studying engineering and biology at the State University of New York at Stony Brook. He planned to be a biomedical engineer, designing devices that help people hear. But then he met whale researchers Roger and Katy Payne.

The Paynes lived on a remote beach in Argentina, studying the right whales that live offshore. They invited Clark to work with them for three months. Clark ended up returning again and again over several years. Once he heard the whales, he was hooked. "In Argentina there would be these breathtaking and almost indescribable days when we would be out on the cliffs along the bay, with the wind blowing, and the whales cavorting below us, and the albatrosses flying above," Clark says. "I was just totally in love with the world. Those kinds of moments are so captivating that it makes me willing to tolerate slaving away in a laboratory for months at a time, just to get out there again."

The Paynes were the first people to recognize that humpback whales actually sing songs. Scientists already knew that whales, like other animals, call to one another. Calls are short, simple sequences

Humpback Whale Song

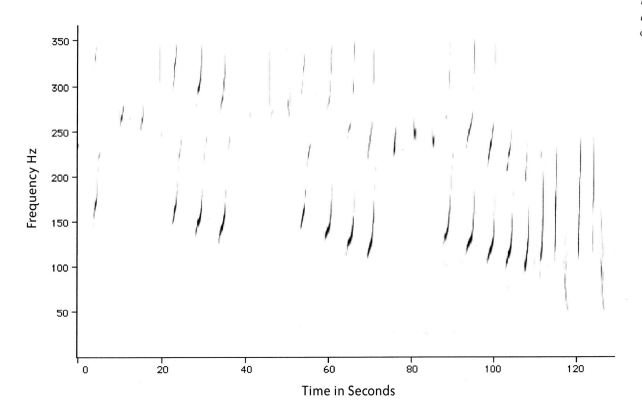

Humpback whale songs contain groups of notes and patterns, just like human songs, as can be seen in this spectrogram.
COURTESY OF CHRISTOPHER W. CLARK

of sounds that occur in certain circumstances such as when a mother calls to a calf and the calf calls back. But male humpback and right whales also make longer, more complicated sounds. By studying these sounds, the Paynes realized the notes whales made came in groups. These groups of notes, called phrases, were repeated. There were patterns—just like melodies in human songs. Whales weren't just calling, they were singing!

A male humpback whale's song can last as long as thirty minutes. He may sing one song after another, for more than twenty-one consecutive hours at a time. And whales seem to listen to each other, because they rarely interrupt one another's songs or calls. Each year, humpback whales in the

A bowhead whale. PHOTO BY GEOFF CARROLL

same groups sing basically the same songs. Over time, they vary the sounds a little, like a jazz singer improvises on a theme. By the next year, the favorite tune has changed somewhat, but all the whales in that area sing it.

Scientists now believe that male whales sing songs to attract females and intimidate other males. But scientists still do not know exactly how whales make these sounds. A whale doesn't open his mouth to sing. The sounds seem to come from his *entire head* and air does not escape from his mouth or blowhole! How the sound is created is just one of the many questions that need to be answered about whales.

Voices Beneath the Ice: Bowheads

Bowhead whales—so called for their huge arched heads—are some of the most vocal whales. As a graduate student, in 1979 Clark joined a research team that studied bowhead whales in the Arctic, near Barrow, Alaska. The scientists hoped to census, or count, bowhead whales by listening to their calls.

Clark and the other researchers pitched their tents on the eight-foot-thick ice that covers the Arctic Ocean in winter. It was like trying to live in a freezer, on top of the ice cube tray. The temperature often reached −40°F. Sheets of ice shifted and collided as the ocean moved and winds blew, forming lumpy, thirty-foot-tall ridges. At times, Clark had to use picks, ropes, and harnesses to climb the ice ridges and rappel down them. The scientists chopped holes in the ice to lower hydrophones into the water. It was hard work.

Bundled up in a coat, hat, and scarf, Clark did not see much except ice and sky, and he didn't hear much except the wind and his own breathing—no birds calling, dogs barking, sirens screaming, or trucks passing. So the first time Clark lowered a hydrophone through a hole in the ice into the water, he was amazed by the life he heard beneath the surface. "I put the hydrophone in the water, and . . . voilá . . . it was like a jungle down there!" he recalls. "The seals were trilling and screaming and the ice was growling, and the whales were singing. Wow, it was a whole discovery."

Clark and other researchers locate bowhead whales by their sounds. They lower hydrophones into several holes about a kilometer apart along the ice edge. Each hydrophone records sounds, noting exactly when each sound is heard. A whale's sound reaches each hydrophone at a slightly different time, so, by using a computer and a little geometry, the scientists can pinpoint where a whale is.

Hearing whales is important because it can be difficult to count them by sight alone. Whales spend a lot of time under water and ice, so an observer cannot see all of them from a boat. However, listening doesn't give a perfect count either, because sometimes the whales are quiet. So to make a good count, scientists need to listen *and* look for them. Research on bowhead whales has

Left: *Christopher Clark sweeps the area near his tent on the ice covering the Arctic Ocean.*
PHOTO COURTESY OF CHRISTOPHER W. CLARK

Right: *Christopher Clark holds a hydrophone (an underwater microphone) before lowering it through a hole to listen for bowhead whales at Point Barrow, Alaska.*
PHOTO COURTESY OF CHRISTOPHER W. CLARK

Counting whales by sight from his perch atop the Arctic ice, Clark helps make the census by sound more accurate.

shown that there were more whales than previously thought. In fact, their population seems to be increasing.

While Clark's whale studies are answering some questions, they are raising others. Bowheads seem to coordinate their movements with one another by calling back and forth as they swim under the ice. Clark wonders what else the calls might mean. "At this time all we can say is that they use calls to communicate simple messages," Clark says. "However, from watching whales for so many years, and living with groups of recognizable individual whales for months at a time, I have grown to believe that they are saying much more than 'I am hungry' or 'I am over here' or 'Let's mate.' I believe they can recognize each other as individuals and can understand subtle messages from each other's voices. Such communication could help them avoid predators, fighting, or wasting energy. It may help them increase their chances of finding food or locating their relatives."

Studies of bowhead whales continue. But Clark is working on other projects, too. Lately he has been studying whales near Hawaii, focusing on how whales use sound to communicate and find their way through the ocean.

Clark's schooling as an engineer has not gone to waste. At times he has to build special instruments to measure and record sound. It's one of his favorite parts of the job. "That's where you get to be creative and work with engineers and mechanics and all kinds of innovative people . . . people who have taught themselves, in their garage, how to build things," Clark says. "And you build little gizmos that you can use on the bottom of the ocean or in the jungle."

Recently, Clark and other scientists developed a device known as a "pop-up"—a seventeen-inch-wide glass bubble that contains audio recording equipment and a signaling device. The device is lowered into the ocean, where it remains for many months, held down by an anchor of sandbags as it records the calls of whales, seals, and other creatures. Then, when the scientists return, they send a signal down to the device, commanding it to burn a fuse and break its connection with the anchor. The sphere "pops up" to the surface and floats, sending out a radio signal and flashes of light to help the scientists locate it. They hoist it into the boat and recover the data from the pop-up's recorder. So far the pop-up has been used off the coasts of California, Hawaii, North Carolina, Massachusetts, and Mexico.

Super Secret Sounds: From Submarines to Whales

For decades, while scientists have been listening for whales, the U.S. Navy has been listening to ocean sounds, too. In the 1950s, during the Cold War, the navy began building a secret underwater network of microphones by draping cables along the bottom of the ocean. On the cables were football-sized clusters of hydrophones. These hydrophones, all over the northern Atlantic and northern Pacific Oceans, listened in on what was happening under water. Together all the hydrophones showed a picture of sound in the ocean, the way Doppler radar, on television weather-casts, shows a picture of clouds in the sky.

By 1992, the relationship between the United States and the countries of the former Soviet Union had improved and Russian submarines were less of a threat. So the navy offered scientists the chance to use navy hydrophones to study underwater earthquakes and volcanoes.

The navy asked Clark to find out whether the underwater listening systems could be used to study whales. One day, he was escorted to a secret, high-security location in a low-ceilinged room about the size of a high school gymnasium. Navy personnel scurried around with notepads. Charts of the ocean hung on the walls. Clark describes it as a dim place, like a house made of cement. Yet it was where he experienced one of his most exciting moments as a scientist.

Clark worked to develop this device, known as a "pop-up." It allows scientists to leave a microphone and recording device in the ocean for months at a time to record the calls of whales. The pop-up rises to the ocean's surface on command. PHOTO BY CAROL "KRILL" CARSON

17

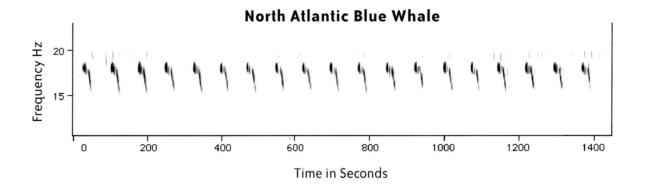

North Atlantic Blue Whale

Time in Seconds

Rows and rows of machines called sound spectrographs were printing out strips of paper called spectrograms. Spectrograms illustrate sound, the way notes and lines in a musical score depict music. They chart how the frequency of a sound changes over time.

Clark's voice still gets emotional as he describes what he saw. "I was looking at these printouts, and I saw a series of notes that looked like commas. The navy people called them commas. I said, 'That's a whale!'"

For years, because of limited funding, Clark had been working with information from, at best, a dozen hydrophones, mostly in shallow water, near shore. Suddenly, looking at the rows of machines, he had information from thousands of hydrophones in deep water all over the Atlantic and northern Pacific Oceans. For Clark it was as if he had climbed a high hill and seen the view from valley to valley. He could suddenly get information about whales singing *all over the ocean.*

By looking at spectrograms, Clark can tell what species a whale is. But it is hard to tell individual whales apart. Once in a while, however, a whale has a really unusual call that is easy to identify. Clark and his navy colleague Lieutenant Chuck Gagnon tracked one such whale, nicknamed "Ol' Blue." By looking at readouts from the machines, they could see where Old Blue was swimming on a given day. The whale swam from Cape Cod to Bermuda to Florida and back to Bermuda over the course of six weeks.

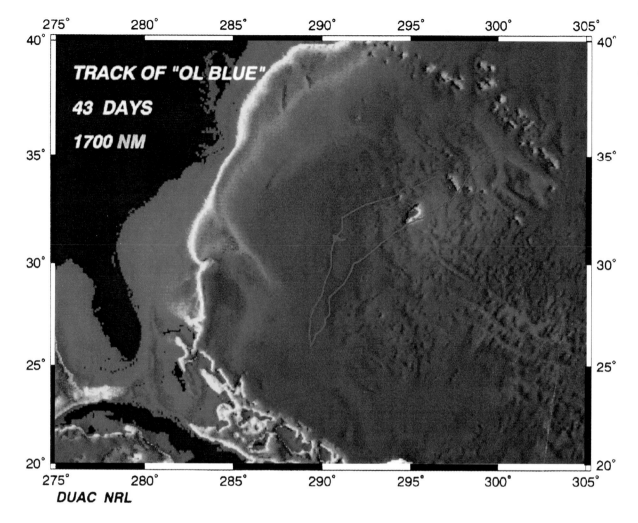

TRACK OF "OL BLUE"

43 DAYS

1700 NM

DUAC NRL

Christopher Clark, working with navy colleagues, tracked Ol' Blue's travels by the calls it made as it swam in the Atlantic Ocean.
COURTESY OF CLYDE NISHIMURA, NAVAL RESEARCH LAB

As a scientist, Clark learned a lot from the navy and the machines. But he helped the navy, too. The people operating the machines started asking him to come look at some of the sound patterns they were finding. In the past, the navy had misidentified some of the sounds they had heard. For instance, some very long, very low sounds were thought to be tiny snapping shrimp. But Clark knew that those sounds came from blue whales, the largest animals on Earth! Some sounds were very

Two right whales greet each other. Will more noise in the ocean interfere with whale communication? PHOTO BY CHRISTOPHER W. CLARK

repetitive and mechanical-sounding, and the navy thought they came from ships exploring for oil and gas. Clark taught them that those sounds were actually made by fin whales calling to one another.

Clark and the navy scientists became friends, working together to understand the sounds in the ocean. He hopes there will be funding to pursue more of these studies. Over the years, the navy did not keep the scrolls of tape they recorded unless they indicated the presence of submarines. Thanks to Clark and other scientists the navy is now keeping many years of data for further study.

Too Noisy for Whales?

Recently, Clark's studies have become increasingly linked to conservation. "I don't think I could be a scientist if I did not also apply my scientific abilities toward conservation," he says. One issue he's been studying is whether noises made by human activities in the ocean harm whales.

Ironically, one source of noise is scientific research. Oceanographers, scientists who study the ocean, have been using loud sound to measure water temperature. (Sound travels faster in warm water than in cold water.) Ocean temperature is important because it affects weather and climate, including El Niños and La Niñas, and it is a good indicator of global warming.

The oceanographers generate an underwater sound in one part of the ocean and measure how long it takes to reach other parts of the ocean. This exercise allows them to measure temperature throughout an entire ocean. A transmitter they installed eighty-five kilometers west of San Fran-

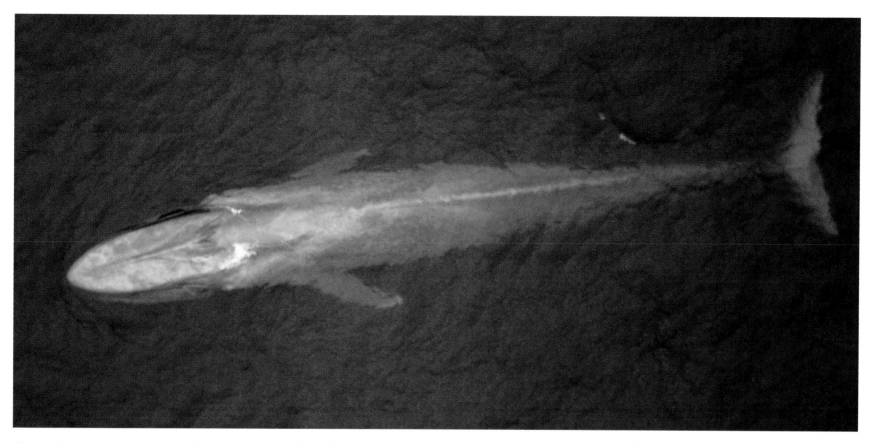

Blue whales are baleen whales. PHOTO BY JIM CUBBAGE, CASCADIA RESEARCH COLLECTIVE

cisco, almost 1,000 meters under water, made a loud, low-pitched rumbling sound that was detected by listening devices near New Zealand, Hawaii, and other places around the North Pacific.

When this research began, many scientists were concerned that the underwater noise might disturb whales, who rely on sound for communication and navigation. Clark and Dr. Adam S. Frankel, another bioacoustic researcher at Cornell, investigated whether the behavior of whales changed because of the rumbling noises. They found that the new noises are not as bad a problem as noises from commercial ships, recreational boats, and oil drilling and exploration.

Conservationists, however, are concerned about the combined impact of all these human-made underwater noises. None of these noises was present during the millions of years when the whales were evolving a way of life that depends on sound. Biologist Katy Payne says, "I have a dim attitude toward all increases of human noise in the ocean. It can only add up to increasing trouble for other species."

In particular, she is worried about the U.S. Navy's decision to make enormously powerful sounds in the ocean in order to find submarines. These sounds are louder than the ones used by scientists to study ocean temperatures. The navy is now funding studies to research the impact of sound in the ocean to determine whether or not their technology is harmful to whales and other marine animals.

Clark is continuing his whale studies. The more Clark learns about whales, the more he is concerned about other ocean-wide problems like pollution and overfishing, as well as noise. He believes that any plans for marine sanctuaries or ocean treaties must take into account how far whales travel as part of their normal lives.

"Recently, through the generosity of the U.S. Navy, I have confirmed Roger Payne's earlier prediction that whales can communicate over many hundreds, if not thousands, of miles," says Clark. "They feed throughout large areas of the ocean and communicate over distances that are sometimes beyond imagination. An entire ocean is their home, not some bay or inlet."

Listening to the Shape of the Ocean

Clark feels sure that whales can sense more than people think they can. Scientists already know that whales use sound not only to communicate but also to find out about their environment. Toothed

Christopher Clark loves his time researching at sea. PHOTO BY JANET DOHERTY

whales, such as beluga whales and orcas, use echolocation, as bats do. The orcas and belugas make clicking noises that bounce off objects. How quickly the echoes from the sounds return to their ears tells them how far away something is and where it is located.

Clark also studies larger whales, called baleen whales. Baleen whales feed by straining small creatures out of the water through a comblike material called baleen. Humpback whales, blue whales, and fin whales are all baleen whales. Clark does not believe that baleen whales use echolocation. But he does wonder if baleen whales, by listening to the reverberations of sounds around them, form some sort of mental picture of ocean features such as underwater mountains, shelves, and the edges of continents.

People can use their senses in a similar way. Even with your eyes closed, by listening to the sounds around you, you can probably tell whether you are in a small room, a big auditorium, or the Grand Canyon. A person's voice out on the street sounds different than when they are in a cave.

Can a whale sense the shape of an ocean by what it hears? No one knows yet. As Clark says, "You don't know that the animals are doing it, but everything tells you that it is physically possible. I make these leaps of faith. . . . They (whales) have lived thirty million years in the ocean. . . . Don't you think that they can do a lot of things that we are just now figuring out they do?"

For now, Clark will keep wondering, and shaping new questions to study. He wouldn't want to be doing anything else. "It is a wonderful feeling to have a career that you totally believe in and that gives you immense satisfaction," he explains. "The satisfaction comes from knowing that I am constantly in the world of discovery, where I am encouraged to use my imagination, creativity, and intelligence for the purpose of learning about life in all its incredible forms."

Curious About Sound? Try a Listening Experiment

Can you "see" with sound? Try this experiment. Choose a partner to walk with you to make sure you don't run into things. Close your eyes and walk down a hallway, such as a hallway in a school. Listen carefully. Can you tell when you are passing the door to a classroom? Can you tell if the door is open or closed, just by the sound? You are sensing the shape and the features of your environment, just by listening. Christopher Clark wonders if whales might do the same kind of sensing by listening to sounds in the ocean.

Something in the Elephants' Silence

Katy Payne

Deep in a rain forest in the Central African Republic, elephant expert Katy Payne writes to family and friends: "I am in Mya's and my field house, writing by lantern light and the glow of my computer. . . . Beyond us the night is full of insect calls—some crickety, others unfamiliar—distant frogs, an owl, and beyond that a deep peaceful silence except for every now and then an elephant rumble or roar . . ."

Payne has spent most of her life doing just this: listening. As a child, she loved music—from folk songs to classical, especially Bach. She majored in music in college. But instead of pursuing a tradi-tional music career, she went on to become a scientist studying animal sound.

For fifteen years Katy Payne and her husband, Roger Payne, stud-ied whale song in the Pacific and northern Atlantic Oceans. (Whale scientist Christopher Clark was one of Roger's students.) The Paynes' base camp for studying humpback whales was a remote beach in

Argentina where they lived and raised their children. When the Payne children grew up, Roger continued studying whales. But Katy decided she wanted a new project all her own.

Katy Payne knew that elephants, like whales, live in family groups and have complex behaviors, so she thought she might like to study them. In 1984, to get a feel for elephants and their lives, she arranged to spend a week with the elephants at the Washington Park Zoo in Portland, Oregon. During that week, she sat outside the elephants' pen. She watched and listened to them. She heard the elephants rumble, trumpet, bellow, snuffle, and growl as they interacted with one another.

On the plane home from Oregon to New York, the vibration of the airplane reminded her of the way the air had sometimes felt near the elephants. She'd felt the same thing as a child, listening to a pipe organ in a church. The organist had played lower and lower notes, until her ears could not hear the notes clearly, but her body could feel the shuddering vibrations. *Perhaps the elephants were making hidden sounds too*, she thought. *Maybe they were making infrasound.*

Infrasound is any sound with a frequency below twenty hertz. That is below the range of sound that people's ears can hear. Lower-frequency sounds, such as infrasound, can be received easily only by a big surface. The human eardrum is too small. Yet the human diaphragm, the muscular membrane just below the ribs, shakes in response to infrasound. Scientist Bill Barklow likens the feeling of infrasound to standing at a parade when the bass drum comes by and makes your body shake.

Top: *Katy and Roger Payne at their whale study site. (Katy and Roger are carrying the back of the boat.)* PHOTO BY LYSA LELAND
Bottom: *Katy Payne checks her battery and tape recorder in Etosha National Park, Namibia.* PHOTO BY JEN AND DES BARTLETT

A female elephant's call, shown in this spectrogram, shows regular patterns.

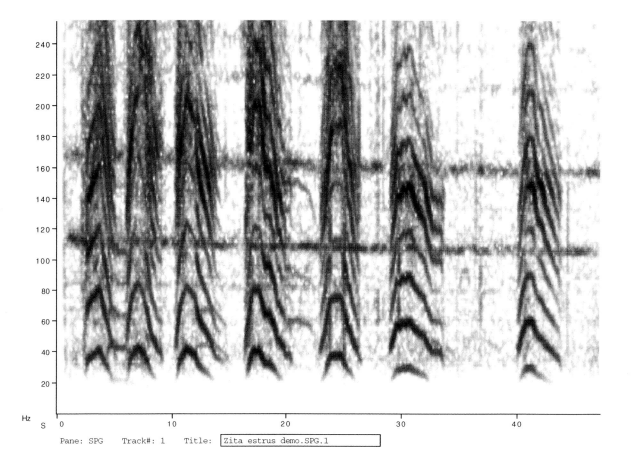

Pane: SPG   Track#: 1   Title: Zita estrus demo.SPG.1

Scientists know that fin whales and blue whales make infrasound. But no one before Katy Payne had realized that land animals might be able to make infrasound, too. People had always wondered how male and female elephants found each other across the great distances of the African savanna. And sometimes elephant herds seemed to react to one another's activities—even when those activities were happening miles away.

The idea that elephants were "talking" without people hearing them was exciting. But Payne wasn't sure she was right. She needed proof. So she borrowed special equipment that could measure infrasound, and, with biologist Bill Langbauer and friend Elizabeth Marshall Thomas, Payne returned to the zoo to study the elephant sounds. They spent a month recording sounds in the elephant enclosures and taking notes on the elephants' behavior.

The tape recorders they used recorded sounds at very slow speeds. Later on, the scientists could play the tapes at regular speed or high speed to raise the pitch of the calls. (The same thing happens when a recording of a person's voice is played at a high speed—it sounds higher and squeakier, like a chipmunk chirping.) Raising the pitch of infrasonic elephant calls makes an even bigger difference. At normal speeds, the calls are so low in pitch that people can't hear them. But at high speeds, the sounds can be heard clearly.

When the team returned home from a month of recording elephant sounds, they still weren't sure that they'd found infrasound. Back at the lab in Ithaca, Payne and biologist Carl Hopkins hooked up the recordings to a spectrograph, which translated the sounds into dots and dashes, creating spectrograms just like the sound pictures Christopher Clark studies for whale research. Payne played part of a seemingly silent recording that had been made when she had felt vibrations in the air. The machine showed the recording was full of calls! Played at high speed, the infrasonic calls sounded like cows mooing. It was the first time anyone had heard elephants communicating in this way. Payne had found something extraordinary.

Cracking the Code

During the sixteen years since the discovery of elephant infrasound, Payne has continued studying elephants calling, both in zoos and in the wild. She formed the Elephant Listening Project at Cornell University's Lab of Ornithology's Bioacoustics Research Program. As part of her research Payne has spent years analyzing tapes and video recordings to figure out which elephants are giving which calls. Linking calls to callers is difficult. Elephants don't necessarily open their mouths or flap their ears when they are calling. And they don't always move when they hear something.

Payne also watches the videos to see what the elephants were doing when they were calling. She

That Noise Makes Me Sick!

Some infrasound actually moves the listener's internal organs, making them shake. Very strong infrasound could make you feel sick, similar to seasickness. Although you wouldn't get sick from hearing an elephant's infrasonic calls, the U.S. Army is investigating ways to use more powerful infrasonic pulses to break up riots. The police or military would play the infrasounds, which would nauseate people nearby and make them want to leave the area. This would disperse the crowd. Once the people left the area and the source of the sound, they would feel better.

Infrasound can travel several miles, allowing widely separated elephant groups to communicate with one another. PHOTO BY KATY PAYNE

and other scientists hope to create an "elephant dictionary" of what each call means. Figuring this out is challenging. Infrasonic elephant calls can travel for miles. A scientist may watch elephants close by, looking for reactions to the calls, but the most interesting reaction may be from an elephant miles away, out of the scientist's view. "It's a trick and a half to figure out what this communication is all about," says Payne.

Nevertheless, scientists have begun to decode some of the calls. Trumpeting, the loud sound elephants make, is used in times of excitement, when elephants are playing, fighting, or alarmed by a predator such as a lion. A special humming call is made by mother elephants when they are near their newborns. Female elephants, when trying to attract a mate, make a low-pitched call that can last for up to forty-five minutes.

"We are beginning to understand what they are saying to each other . . . we can draw some conclusions. This is terribly exciting," says Payne.

Katy Payne shares her love of elephants with a group of fifth-graders in her hometown of Ithaca, New York. PHOTO BY JANE MOON CLARK

Counting Elephants and Conserving Them

Payne is not just a scientist. She is an environmentalist who feels a deep connection with the creatures she studies. The major threats to the survival of elephants are loss of habitat and poaching—illegal hunting. But elephants Payne has studied have died in other ways, too. In 1991, elephants in the families she was studying in Zimbabwe were shot and killed. These elephants, who lived in a park, were not poached. They were "culled"—killed by hunters hired by park officials to reduce the number of elephants.

Unlike parks elsewhere, these parks had large populations of elephants because the parks were well protected. But many people who had recently moved to regions near the park borders were upset

that their crops were being eaten by the elephants. Elephants were not welcome outside the park as they had been in the old days. And when confined to a small area, even a park, elephants can become destructive, so park officials hired hunters to kill some of them to reduce the population.

Payne recognizes that elephant overpopulation in some parks is a valid concern, but she rejects culling as the solution. Elephants have complex social lives. "Elephants suffer, perhaps as much as people do, when friends and family members are killed," says Payne. She discusses her views on culling in her 1998 book, *Silent Thunder: In the Presence of Elephants.* When that book was released, Payne spent most of her time giving talks and interviews to spread her conservation message. She was deluged by inquiries from the press for information on her scientific discoveries and on the

View of Dzanga Bai, the clearing in the Central African Republic where Katy Payne studied elephants. PHOTO BY KATY PAYNE

controversial subject of culling. "Some people felt it was irresponsible of me to take such a strong stand against culling," she says. "But you have to speak out about what you care about."

In Pursuit of Forest Elephants

Payne's love of science and convictions about conservation finally brought her story full circle in 1999. That was when she realized that studies of elephants' calls might be helpful in counting the number of elephants. A better count of wild elephants is useful because conservationists must prove elephants are rare or decreasing in number in order to convince governments to take action to protect elephants. Payne was particularly interested in finding out how many elephants

Members of the Central African Republic research team (left to right: *Melissa, Mya, Melebu, and Koto) videotape elephants from the platform.* PHOTO BY KATY PAYNE

lived in the forests of central and western Africa. These elephants are almost never seen because they live among thick bushes and trees. Recently, scientists determined that these forest elephants are a separate species from savanna elephants, which live in the more open spaces of East Africa.

For many years the only way to estimate elephant numbers has been to count their droppings. Payne wanted to see if she could estimate their numbers by listening to their calls. To study this problem, she traveled to the Central African Republic with Steve Gulick, Mya Thompson, and Melissa Groo. The expedition, based at Andrea Turkalo's research site, was one of the highlights of her career. She describes the experience in her letters:

> This morning we set up house, shop, and study, filled four batteries with acid, and got the solar panels charging them. Then we entered the forest, which I believe is primeval. A winding red sand path led us below huge buttressed trees. . . . A large gorilla's footprints ran before us all. Coming out on a swamp we waded for a quarter-hour waist-deep in a rapidly flowing cool stream, then entered a deeper forest where we were surrounded by African grey parrots singing lusciously . . .

After quite a long time I suddenly had the sense that we were approaching an opening. A flight of wooden steps appeared on the path before us. Running up we found ourselves on a huge thatch-roofed platform overlooking the most breathtakingly ideal place for the study of elephants that I could possibly imagine.

We set down our loads—the first of many—and sat shaded on wooden benches, with a little breeze wafting over us to watch forty elephants, young, old, female and male, involved in a dozen different elephantish behaviors.

Payne and the research team used a computer and microphones in the field to view elephant sounds that were sometimes too low for the researchers to hear. PHOTO BY KATY PAYNE

Payne and the others began to set up their equipment on, under, and around the thatch-roofed platform that had been built by previous expeditions. From there Payne could look out over an opening in the forest. This opening was a special gathering place for forest elephants, who often visited to wade in the mud holes that formed there.

The first question for the scientists was where to place the microphones and recording devices. Initially, they thought about putting the microphones in trees, but they were concerned that monkeys or elephants might pull them down. They settled for burying the microphones and recording devices in abandoned termite mounds.

Having several microphones in different locations was necessary to pinpoint where calls were coming from. By registering when sounds reached each microphone, computers could calculate where the sounds originated. Computers also created spectrograms of the elephant calls. Meanwhile, video cameras recorded the elephants' activity. All this equipment was powered by solar cells.

Payne's research had its challenges. For weeks there was heavy rainfall. The scientists' clothes, papers, and food began to mold. Bugs crept in. The scientists had to work constantly to keep all the equipment running. There was also a unique camp pest she mentions in her letters:

Cheeky, a young male elephant, on one of his many visits to the camp. In front of the cabin is a solar panel that generated electricity for the researchers' equipment. PHOTO BY KATY PAYNE

P.S. A beautiful young bull elephant whom Andrea has named "Cheeky" digs holes in the dirt floor of the kitchen each night and eats Andrea's tomato plants. He never disturbs the cutlery or glasses. Yesterday when we arrived home at the end of the day I met him at the outhouse, fanning his huge perfect ears when he leaned down to look in.

Payne's research in the Central African Republic was successful. While there, she was able to study infrasonic calls. About half of the elephant calls recorded by the computer were calls that the scientists themselves couldn't hear. By looking back over the videos of elephant behavior, Payne hopes to understand what these calls mean.

Payne's research also linked the number of calls to the number of elephants. She's still analyzing

Katy Payne observes elephants in the Dzanga Bai clearing in the Central African Republic.
PHOTO BY MELISSA GROO

the data, but it now looks as if elephants can be counted by sounds, as has been done with whales. "This is turning out to be wonderful," Payne says. "If you listen carefully to the calls of an elephant group you can figure out how many there are, and who they are—whether there's a healthy balance of babies, adult males, and females. The calls of elephants open a window on the lives and health of hidden elephant populations." It is hoped that knowing how many elephants live in the forest and where those elephants roam will help conservationists gather support for protecting the habitat elephants need. This news is good for elephants, and it is good for Katy Payne, who has found a way to use her scientific work in the service of conservation.

Sounds in the Night Sky

Bill Evans

While Christopher Clark and Katy Payne seek sounds close to the ground or under water, Bill Evans is looking to the sky. He studies bird calls—not just any bird calls, but the calls birds make while migrating at night.

Millions of birds migrate each year, traveling thousands of miles from their summer breeding grounds to their winter homes. Orioles, tanagers, grosbeaks, warblers, flycatchers, and hummingbirds seen in the United States in summer are mostly "neotropical migrants." They fly to and from the tropics, the areas near the equator. More than eighty percent of them journey at night.

Evans wants to track these travelers. He would like to set up a continent-wide program that would let scientists know where and when the birds are traveling. This information could be used to pinpoint and preserve areas that are important to the birds' survival. "The sooner you can document a population's decline," Evans says, "the more efficient you can be in doing something about the problem."

Evans's interest in night migration began in 1985. At the time he was doing various part-time jobs, including delivering pizza, unloading trucks for United Parcel Service, and working at a library.

His main interest was the history of science, particularly the history of electricity, but he was also an avid birdwatcher.

One May night, walking to a campsite in Minnesota, he heard something in the sky. It was the short, sharp calls of birds migrating overhead. Evans lay down on a hillside and listened to the calls. "I was totally amazed at the number and the variety of calls," he says. That night brought Evans his big idea, an idea that has driven his life ever since. "I thought then that if I had a tape recorder I could record those sounds and link them to the number of birds flying over, and that might be important for conservation. I had this vision that you could use computers to automatically detect and identify these calls and track bird migration."

The next day, Evans started hunting for good recording equipment and began recording bird calls at night. One challenge was eliminating other calls from his recordings. "There are a lot of strange sounds in the night, and you don't know what some of the sounds are," says Evans. When he sets up a recording station, he makes sure it's far away from bushes and trees, to avoid crickets and other insects. The night-flight calls of warblers and sparrows sound a lot like cricket chirps,

Left: *Bill Evans tries to identify the sounds migrating birds make when they fly overhead at night. Here he listens on a hilltop above Ithaca, New York.* PHOTO BY TIM W. GALLAGHER

Right: *This yellow-rumped warbler is one of the many birds that migrate at night. These warblers migrate 300 to 6,000 miles from their summer homes in Canada and the United States to their winter homes in the southern United States, Mexico, Central America, the Caribbean, and South America.*
PHOTO BY JEFF SAYRE AND APRIL PULLEY SAYRE

Bill Evans checks his recording equipment at one of his stations, a barn in upstate New York.
PHOTO BY TIM GALLAGHER

and although a chorus of insects in the background won't ruin a recording, a few crickets right near the microphone can.

After a few years of recording bird calls whenever he had time off, Evans went to work at the Library of Natural Sounds at Cornell, where he searched through their collection of bird calls. He found that no one had investigated the night-flight calls of birds. "I realized at that point that I was going to have to go out and figure out the identity of these calls on my own."

Evans left his full-time job at the lab so he could have time to pursue his research plans. He took short-term work, here and there, on scientific research projects run by others. All the while, he was doing his own research on night migration.

Who's Calling? The Hunt for Clues

Recording the sounds birds made at night wasn't difficult. The problem, for Evans, was identifying the calls he heard. Tracing the identity of the calls led him on a ten-year, continent-wide search for clues.

First he studied the daytime calls of birds east of the Rocky Mountains. It turned out that birds do sometimes sing their "night flight" calls during the day, but they're not the common bird calls that most people know. Evans had to study the wide range of calls the birds made each day to find ones that matched the sounds he heard at night. Even then, he was able to identify only a few calls, and he could only guess at the others. He needed more clues.

Evans's next puzzle-solving strategy was to record night-flight calls in different places. He had

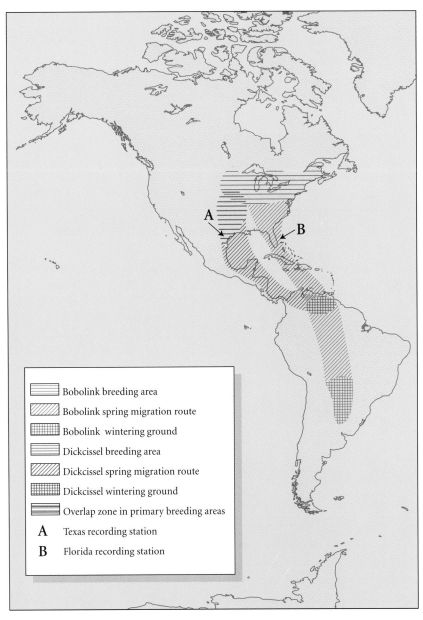

Daytime sightings of bobolinks and dickcissels allowed birdwatchers to construct the range map above. Evans used range maps like this one as clues to figure out the identities of nighttime bird calls. COURTESY OF BILL EVANS

Legend:
- Bobolink breeding area
- Bobolink spring migration route
- Bobolink wintering ground
- Dickcissel breeding area
- Dickcissel spring migration route
- Dickcissel wintering ground
- Overlap zone in primary breeding areas
- A Texas recording station
- B Florida recording station

already recorded calls in Minnesota and in New York State. For several years he recorded calls in Florida, Texas, and Alabama. These were his sets of data.

He listened to the tapes and noted which were the most common calls and the least common calls in each place. Then he found out what were the most common and least common migrating birds in each area. (Birdwatchers know which birds are common because they see some of the migrating birds resting in the area during the day.)

Evans explains how he cross-matched calls to identify them. "For example, the bobolink, in spring migration, is a very rare migrant in Texas, but a very common migrant in Florida. So that was an easy one. If I got a common call note in Florida, I would know it would be one of the common migrants that people probably see on the ground during the day in Florida." Evans then searched through his recordings of daytime calls to confirm his suspicions about which calls were which.

More than two hundred species of night-migrating birds live east of the Rocky Mountains, and some of these birds give more than a dozen different kinds of calls. So Evans was working with many different pieces of information at one time. "It was like working out a big jigsaw puzzle. I had these circumstantial clues, and they all sort of gelled." He worked with another bird-call enthusiast, Michael O'Brien of Cape May, New Jersey, to create an audio field guide to the night calls of birds. "You can't know any one with certainty, until you know them all," Evans explains.

Figuring out the identity of the night-flying birds was only part of

Bobolink Diurnal Flight Call — Florida

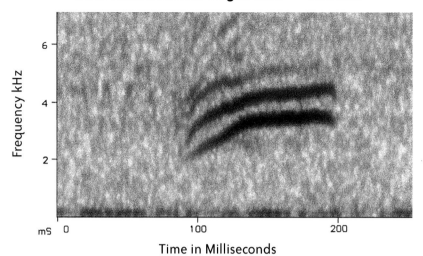

Presumed Bobolink Night Flight Call

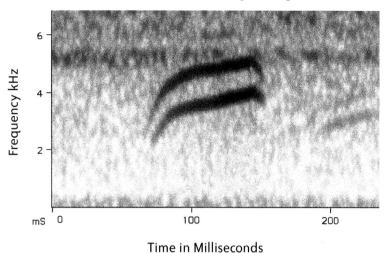

Daytime and nighttime calls may be similar, but they are not exactly the same.
COURTESY OF BILL EVANS

Evans's plan. His next challenge was to find a computer program that could identify and count these calls. That was tricky because the program had to be able to tell whether only one bird was calling or several of the same species were calling. The software for this work is only partly developed. Bird calls are being detected and counted at sites in Minnesota, New York, and Texas. But so far, the calls of only a few species can be clearly identified by the computer.

Who Cares What Birds Are Saying?

Studying bird calls has some surprising applications. While doing his own research, Evans has supported himself by working on a variety of other research projects. For instance, Evans conducted a study to find and count willow flycatchers along the Colorado River near the Arizona border. These rare birds live along rivers in thickets of bushes twelve to fifteen feet tall, so it's hard to walk through the area and see the birds. "Once you're in the thickets, you can't see anything," says Evans. "And it's filled with rattlesnakes."

Bobolinks, which live in prairies, have a call that sounds a lot like the noises of R2D2, the robot in Star Wars. *Sounds for these and other fictional movie robots and monsters are often made by mixing together or distorting the recordings of real animal calls.*
PHOTO BY B. HENRY, COURTESY OF VIREO-ANSP

Despite the difficulties, scientists need to find out how many flycatchers live along the rivers so they can monitor whether the population is increasing or decreasing. Willow habitats along rivers are becoming scarce. People often cut willow trees down so that cattle can easily reach the river water. This leaves fewer homes for willow flycatchers. Several projects are under way to restore streamside habitats, allowing the willows to regrow. Would these projects help restore willow flycatcher populations? To find out, Evans needed to know how many willow flycatchers lived in these kinds of areas.

Evans came up with a way to count the willow flycatchers. He built a helium balloon out of a big plastic dropcloth and hung microphones, a recorder, and a transmitter from the bottom of the balloon. Then he and his assistants filled the balloon with helium so it would float over the brushy area. A global positioning system (GPS) receiver on the balloon mapped where it floated. Evans and his assistants retrieved the recorder and listened to the tape to figure out how many willow flycatchers were calling in that area.

A Growing Sense of Mission: Tower Kills

Recently, Evans has been doing research projects that are more closely related to his night-migration research. In 1996, the United States Fish and Wildlife Service wanted to find out which birds migrate over a certain area of north-central Nebraska at night. They needed this information because an electric power company was considering building a wind farm there. A wind farm is a large area of land covered with dozens, sometimes hundreds, of wind turbines. These turbines, which look like windmills, convert wind energy into electricity. But migrating birds sometimes run into these turbines and are killed. In the western United States, golden eagles and hawks have been found dead under turbines. So the power company, under a directive from the U.S. Fish and Wildlife Service, hired Evans to use his acoustic monitoring technique to find out what songbirds might be endangered as they flew through that area at night.

The balloon carries the recording device over the willow thicket, and Evans tracks the equipment with a radiowave transmitter and receiver. PHOTOS BY BRIAN O'SHEA

Evans's recordings were initially meant just to survey what species migrated over the proposed turbine area. But the recordings documented much more. While he was there, he made recordings of night-migrating birds near another kind of tall structure: a 317-foot radio tower in the area. "The most striking result was that I had recorded some birds actually colliding with the radio tower during their night migration," Evans explains. "In one recording you can hear the wingbeats of what sounds like a duck, then a loud collision sound, and then a thud on the ground. A blue-winged teal was found dead under the tower the next day."

Evans was startled and deeply concerned about what he found in his research. "What really opened my eyes was how many alarm calls I recorded. Many flocks of ducks that were migrating at night sounded like they came upon the radio tower and at the last minute realized it was there and swerved to avoid the tower, often giving alarm calls. It was the experience of listening to my tape recordings made under the 317-foot radio transmission tower in Nebraska that motivated me to become an activist in preventing bird mortality at towers."

Tall structures, clearly, have an impact on migrating birds. That's true whether the structures are towers, wind turbines, or buildings. Evans found that many songbirds do migrate through the area of the proposed wind farm, and they fly at altitudes lower than the tops of the turbines would be. But Evans's studies of other wind farms have indicated that the impact on small birds such as songbirds is minimal. Some may be killed, but not large numbers.

Evans's personal conclusions about wind farms are generally positive. He's studied wind farms in several areas. The turbines are good because wind energy is clean energy: wind farms do not produce the air pollution that coal-powered plants do. But wind farms do cause trouble for birds, especially hawks and eagles. Some scientists are also concerned about bats hitting the turbines. For now, Evans believes that wind farms are a good idea as long as the turbines are less than 300 feet high and as long as they are sited carefully, outside major bird migration routes.

After his experience in Nebraska, Evans created a Web site to share information about birds being killed by towers of various kinds. The Web site, www.towerkill.com, explains that many birds are killed by towers that transmit radio, television, and cell phone signals. With cell phone use increasing rapidly, cell phone towers are being put up all over the United States and Europe. Evans is searching for ways to minimize the effect of these towers on migrating birds. He is hoping that citizens will pressure the radio, television, and cell phone industries into considering bird mortality in the design and siting of towers.

A Dinner Plate, Two Flowerpots, and the Future

Evans's activism concerning tower kills is only part of his conservation work. His long-term plan is to get more people involved in tracking migrating birds. Already he has installed microphones on the roofs of eleven Texas high schools. (These high schools are ideal locations because their roofs are big, flat, and away from vegetation.) A cable runs from the microphone down to a computer in each school's science lab. Every day, students can check the computer to see what calls were heard the previous night. They can also reach a Web site to compare their data with that from other schools.

Evans's inexpensive microphones, protected by plastic flowerpots, are on many rooftops already. PHOTO BY BILL EVANS.

People can do this at home, too. Evans has designed an inexpensive receiving dish that people can install on the roof of their house. The device is made of a dinner plate, a hearing-aid microphone, two flowerpots, and plastic wrap. Wires from the microphone/receiver run to a computer that records the sounds each day. Instructions for making the receiver are on Evans's Web site, www.oldbird.org. It takes some tinkering, but once it's installed, people can get up in the morning and check their home computer to see spectrograms of the sounds recorded the previous night.

By matching the spectrograms on the computer with those in a guide to night-flight calls, a person can find out what birds flew over the house during the previous night. Eventually, the software may do this automatically. It already does this matching for a few species, such as dickcissels. Evans is also developing the Web site materials in Spanish so that more people in Central and South America can track birds, too.

Above: *Dickcissels spend the winter in South America and the summer in the prairies of the midwestern United States.*
PHOTO BY A. MORRIS, COURTESY OF VIREO-ANSP

Above right: *Data collected by high schools in Texas is helping Evans understand when dickcissels migrate.* COURTESY OF BILL EVANS

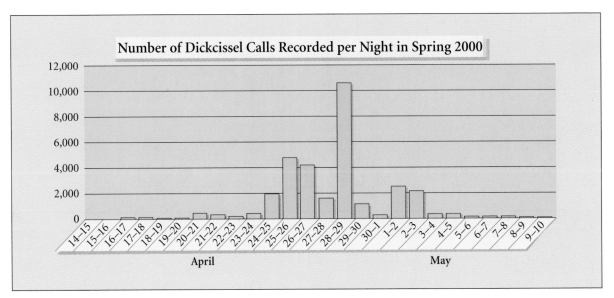

Number of Dickcissel Calls Recorded per Night in Spring 2000

Evans has big plans and big dreams for tracking birds. So far only he and one other person do this work full-time, but he's driven to do his work, and he enjoys it. "One of the neatest things about studying birds in general, compared to studying fields like music or art or computers, is that birds are not manmade," says Evans. "You get to ask these questions: Where do birds come from? Why are they here? You can ask that about a computer—where did they come from, why are they here? And the answer is: well, people designed them, developed them for various purposes, and that is where it ends. But why are birds here? It goes back to the creation, evolution, the mysteries . . . it gets you into a bigger realm of existence."

There are still plenty of unanswered questions for future researchers in the study of night migration. For instance, scientists don't know why migrating birds call at night. "One of the theories is that birds call at night for air traffic control, so they can work out their flight spacing and avoid colliding with one another," says Evans.

Another theory is that some birds fly as families, or in flocks, and call in order to stay together during migration. But these are only unproven theories. "The problem with those theories," Evans

wryly admits, "is that there are whole groups of birds—flycatchers, vireos, catbirds, and orioles—which do not seem to give calls during migration. This is one of the big mysteries right now."

So why should Evans, or anyone else, spend so much time tracking migrating birds? Evans is casting his eye to the future. "My night-flight call monitoring and balloon monitoring work are

Scientists can count birds that migrate during the day, such as these hawks over Panama, by sight alone. But Evans studies night-migrating birds, so he must use sound. PHOTO BY JEFF SAYRE AND APRIL PULLEY SAYRE

Bill Evans listens to migrating birds in the moonlight near Ithaca, New York. PHOTO BY TIM W. GALLAGHER

aimed at leaving a record of bird populations for the future—at instituting new monitoring techniques that will fill gaps in our knowledge. The night-flight call monitoring effort is documenting the night flights of today and archiving this information so folks in the future will have a record to compare with their own observations."

"We can't appreciate what we don't know is there," Evans points out. "By counting songbirds and tracking their populations, we have a powerful means of tracking environmental changes, understanding how our actions are shaping the world, and allowing ourselves to respond in time to keep our ecosystem in balance."

New Technologies, New Voices

The Future of Bioacoustics

It may not take a computer to hear a bird's call or a whale's song, but computers are making it easier to study them. CANARY, a computer program developed by Steve Mitchell and Sean Cunningham, members of Christopher Clark's research team, now allows bioacousticians to process tremendous amounts of information in digital files. They can look at and compare sounds piece by piece, in large batches. Work that took months or even years a decade ago now can be done in a day. CANARY, which was first developed to study whale calls, is now used by Katy Payne to study elephant calls and by Bill Evans to study night-migrating birds.

Clearly, the contribution of a scientist such as Clark is not just the research he does—it's also what he shares. Clark is only one of many scientists who have shared their technological innovations and expertise. Katy and Roger Payne helped train and advise Clark and other bioacousticians early in their careers. Bill Evans, by developing an inexpensive microphone setup, is encouraging countless numbers

Bioacoustic researchers share ideas, help one another, and sometimes clown around! This photo shows the bowhead whale research team at Point Barrow, Alaska. Christopher Clark is lying on the ice. PHOTO BY CHRISTOPHER W. CLARK

of young people to gather data for scientific study. Over the years, bioacousticians have helped one another with everything from equipment to encouragement, from advice to office space, but the most important things they have shared are ideas. Creative ideas, along with new technologies, are stimulating the field of bioacoustics. And these days, bioacousticians are looking for, and finding, animal sounds in some strange places.

Hippos, Above and Below

Bill Barklow is a bioacoustician who studies hippopotamuses. Hippos make sounds above water that people can hear. But scientists did not know that hippos communicated below water until Barklow discovered it.

Barklow's interest in hippos began by accident. In 1986 Barklow went on a wildlife-watching safari in Tanzania. He was on vacation from his usual research—studying the calls of North American water birds called loons. One afternoon when Barklow was watching hippos at a water hole, he began wondering about hippo behavior. "I noticed that the hippos seemed to be making sounds under water," Barklow recalls. "There were sprays—fountains of water that would come up from below water—which could have been sound. Then I noticed that when hippos on the surface called, other hippos nearby would surface. So I was kind of curious. I wondered if the hippos were communicating under water. When I got home, I checked the literature and found that no one had studied this."

Barklow managed to get a small grant, and he returned to Africa with a hydrophone. What he found was thrilling. "I discovered this symphony of underwater sounds that the hippos were making, that I didn't believe anyone had ever heard before," says Barklow. "It was a rush!" He was amazed by the difference in what he was hearing on the hydrophone and what he was hearing in the air.

Since then, Barklow has found out that hippos can broadcast their calls above and below the water at the same time. A hippo, half-submerged, can simultaneously send a call to hippos on shore and hippos in the water.

Barklow not only wants to know about the sounds hippos make; he's also curious about how well they hear. But it's hard to make a wild hippo take a hearing test. A wild hippo won't push a button or raise a hand to tell a tester when it hears a sound. So Barklow and his assistants are working with animal trainers at Busch Gardens in Tampa, Florida, to devise a test. The animal trainers are teaching captive hippos to come to a particular station when they hear a tone. Eventually, Barklow hopes, he can play tones of different types, and if the hippos go to the stations, he will know that the hippos hear the sounds.

Barklow's research is driven primarily by his scientific curiosity. Yet he, like other bioacousticians, would be pleased if his work could contribute to better conservation of the creatures he studies. Wild hippos sometimes attack people. These attacks are a problem in some areas of Africa, especially as the increasing human population encroaches on wild areas. Understanding what hippos' calls and postures mean may help prevent such attacks, protecting both people and hippos. A better understanding of hippos may also help park managers improve plans to provide the habitat hippos need.

Earth-Shaking Animal Sounds

Sound is vibration. Vibrations can travel through almost any medium: air, water, wood, soil, steel, even stems. Dr. Peter M. Narins, of the University of California, studied white-lipped frogs, which half bury themselves in mud while they call to one another. Their calls can be heard through the air, but Narins wondered if the frogs also transmitted sounds through the ground. By using a geophone—a microphone used by geologists to detect seismic tremors that warn of an earthquake—Narins found that they do. When a white-lipped frog calls, a pouch on its throat hits the ground, making a thump that travels through the mud. Other frogs can sense these vibrations.

Bill Barklow sets up his equipment in Africa to study hippos, visible only as lumps in the background. PHOTO BY LYNDA RICHARDSON

Giant kangaroo rats like this one live in the western United States and are not much bigger than domestic gerbils. PHOTO BY JAN RANDALL

Geophones are helping scientist Dr. Jan Randall, too. Randall studies kangaroo rats, nature's natural drummers. Kangaroo rats, which hop on their hind feet like kangaroos, live in burrows in American deserts. The largest ones make dirt mounds where they store seeds, their main food. These mounds are also musical instruments. Now and then, a kangaroo rat will lean forward on its front legs and slap its back feet, both at once, on the ground. It does this over and over, drumming its feet at a rate of almost twenty beats a second. Randall says the sound varies among kangaroo rat species. "When I first heard the desert kangaroo rat, I thought that someone was in the burrow drumming. The other two species of kangaroo rats combine these single foot drums into rolls, and then it sounds more like a drum roll . . . *brrroop, brrroop, brrroop.*" In some species, each rat drums with its own particular rhythm, so the rats can tell one another apart. Kangaroo rats use this drumming to announce their territories and to scare off predators.

Randall also studies wild gerbils in Uzbekistan. Like pet gerbils and kangaroo rats, these wild gerbils foot-drum to communicate. Gerbil drumming can be heard in the air, but the vibrations also travel through the ground, so other gerbils hear it in underground tunnels.

Randall studies both rats and gerbils by recording their foot-drumming and then playing the sounds back to them and watching their reactions. She has also sought the assistance of engineer Ted Lewis, who rigged up a mechanical ground-thumping machine. Now Randall can play a tape of a particular animal's drumming into the machine, and the machine will thump it out into the ground. By using this technique, Randall can ensure that the rats or gerbils will hear her experimental signals not just in the air, but also through the ground.

The ground isn't the only place where scientists are finding animal sounds. Bioacoustic researcher Rex Cocroft has found that thornbugs, stinkbugs, lacewings, and katydids send messages through plant stems. These insects shake the stems with their feet or by vibrating their abdomens. The vibrations travel through the stems, and other insects feel the messages. These sounds may warn of predators, attract mates, or keep insects in contact with one another.

The more scientists know about the sounds animals make, the more questions arise. Today they have more ideas than ever about where to look for animal sounds and what the animals might be saying. They just need the time, space, funding, and help to find the answers.

Getting Involved in Bioacoustics: An Open Door for Creative Minds

Most bioacousticians are eager to share their interest and encourage students to enter the field. Jan Randall says, "I love my job and I am really glad I stuck with it." Randall enjoys training undergraduate and graduate students. "I think that one of my contributions has been as a role model, to women particularly," says Randall. "We have more women students in our department than men.

So I want to tell young women out there that they can be anything they want to be. If they want to be a field biologist, and go out in the desert alone at night, they can do it. There's no limit to what women can do in biology."

Christopher Clark encourages students to get out and study things in person. "You can't experience life by just watching it on a screen," he says. Scientist Katy Payne puts it simply: "Whatever interests you most, keep giving yourself experiences of it, any way you possibly can."

The road to a career in bioacoustics varies. Most bioacousticians earn a Ph.D. in a scientific field. Others, such as Katy Payne and Bill Evans, got into the field by gaining hands-on experience and following their passion. Looking back on how his career has developed, Evans admits he's taken an unusual path. "Basically this night-migration study was a hobby that got out of control," he says. For him, that's part of the fun. "You are not going to make a lot of money studying bioacoustics, but you are going to have a great time. It is a frontier—something that is totally unknown," he says.

Clark encourages students to seek a solid but varied academic background: "The science and conservation of these animals desperately need young, creative minds that are able to move freely between different educational media. So go out and learn about genetics, or toxicology, or population biology, or conservation science. Mix a bunch of different training because it is in the mixing that your mind gets stimulated and you make ingenious connections and come up with novel solutions."

Curiosity and Conservation: A True Calling

Studying animal calls is often fun and exciting, but a lot of the actual work requires tremendous commitment and hours of meticulous and often tedious scientific data analysis. "People who watch nature films on the Discovery Channel do not realize the hundreds

Bill Evans's work may lead to better conservation. PHOTO BY BRIAN O'SHEA

57

of hours of time that go into the scientific research," says Dr. Jan Randall. So why do bioacousticians dedicate their lives to listening to elephants calling, birds chirping, whales singing, or rats thumping their feet on the ground?

Randall simply loves doing scientific research: coming up with hypotheses, gathering data, and testing the hypotheses to see if they were right. She finds the process satisfying. Like many bioacousticians, she is constantly lured by the exciting prospect of discovering something new. She takes advantage of any opportunity to use her science for conservation, as well.

Christopher Clark, who switched from engineering to studying whales, describes his enthusiasm for his career in very personal terms: "I am enamored with the ocean and I love working with these large animals . . . that sing and produce all these marvelous sounds. I'm not interested in picking and poking at things and taking animals apart. I like to just go and listen and observe an animal and use my brain to put it all together."

Clearly, bioacousticians find studying the sounds of animals challenging and deeply rewarding. Each discovery, in the lab or in the field, feeds their curiosity and leads them to new ideas. Their work also gives them a chance to get out into wild forests, savannas, deserts, oceans, and beaches, where they feel connected to the earth.

Environmental concerns help fuel many bioacousticians' work, as well. Bill Evans says, "Having information on songbird populations is important so that people in the future can understand how their actions are shaping the earth." In short, he believes that the more people know about birds, the better chance they have of saving them.

Katy Payne says, "My two deep desires, at the most basic level, are to learn about the experiences of other animals and to help in the conservation of this beautiful earth." Clearly, her goal is shared by many other scientists studying animal sound—whether they spend their days listening to whale songs, insect hums, bird calls, or gerbil foot-drumming. Like so many adults and children, these scientists would love to know what the animals are saying.

PHOTO BY APRIL PULLEY SAYRE

Suggestions for Further Reading and Listening

Books

Leary, Catherine. *Awesome Experiments in Light & Sound.* New York: Sterling Publishers, 1999. (Middle-grade children's book.)

Payne, Katherine. *Elephants Calling.* New York: Crown Publishers, 1992. (Picture book.)

———. *Silent Thunder: In the Presence of Elephants.* New York: Simon & Schuster, 1998.

Payne, Roger. *Among Whales.* New York: Scribners, 1995.

Sabbeth, Alex. *Rubber-Band Banjos and a Java-Jive Bass: Projects and Activities on the Science of Music and Sound.* New York: Wiley & Sons, 1997. (Middle-grade children's book.)

Animal Sound Recordings

Elliott, Lang. *A Guide to Night Sounds.* Ithaca, N.Y.: Naturesound Studio, 1992.

———. *Know Your Bird Sounds. Vols. 1–3.* Ithaca, N.Y.: Naturesound Studio, 1997.

———. *Music of the Birds: A Celebration of Bird Song.* Boston: Houghton Mifflin, 1999.

Elliott, Lang, and Cynthia Page. *The Calls of Frogs and Toads.* Minnetonka, Minn.: NorthWord Audio, 1998.

Stokes, Donald, and Lillian Stokes, with Lang Elliott. *Stokes Field Guide to Bird Songs: Eastern Region.* New York: Time Warner Audio Books, 1997.

Walton, Richard K., and Robert W. Larson. *Birding by Ear.* Boston: Houghton Mifflin, 1999.

Articles

Berger, Cynthia. "Making Sense of the Songs Whales Sing." *National Wildlife,* June/July 1998, 52–60.

Chadwick, Douglas H. "Listening to Humpbacks." *National Geographic,* July 1999, 111–29.

Coppens, Alan B., and James V. Sanders. "Sound." Discovery Channel School, original content provided by World Book Online, www.discoveryschool.com/homeworkhelp/worldbook/atozscience/s/520640.html.

Finnell, Rebecca B. "Symphony Beneath the Sea." *Natural History,* March 1991, 38–76.

Payne, Katherine. "A Change of Tune." *Natural History,* March 1991, 45–46.

———. "Elephant Talk." *National Geographic.* August 1989, 264–77.

Payne, Roger. "Humpbacks: Their Mysterious Songs." *National Geographic,* January 1979, 18–25.

Schwartz, David M. "Snatching Scientific Secrets from the Hippos' Gaping Jaws." *Smithsonian,* March 1996, 90–102.

How You Can Get Involved in Research and Conservation

1. *Whales, Elephants, Birds, and Bioacoustics:* Find out the most up-to-date information about bioacoustic projects. A good place to start is the Web site of Cornell University's Bioacoustics Research Program. They have information on sound recording equipment and ongoing conservation projects that students can join.

Bioacoustics Research Program
Cornell Laboratory of Ornithology
159 Sapsucker Woods Road
Ithaca, NY 14850
www.ornith.cornell.edu/BRP

2. *Night-Migrating Bird Calls:* At www.oldbird.org you can get instructions for building your own microphone. You can set up a night-flight call monitoring station at your home or at your school and then connect with others doing the same via the Oldbird Web site.

Bill Evans's Bird Tracking Site
www.oldbird.org

3. *Animal Calls:* You can get a microphone (or build your own using the instructions on www.oldbird.com) and any recording device (cheap portable cassette player, etc.) and make recordings of insects, frogs, birds, and even your own voice.

To learn to identify what you are recording, check Web sites or CDs of animal calls. For links to animal noise recordings and places to obtain CDs of animal calls, check the author's Web site: www.aprilsayre.com.

4. *Tower Kills:* Research the issues of radio and cell phone towers and their impact on migrating birds. Write to cell phone companies, radio companies, congressional representatives, and others to express your concerns. You can begin your research at Bill Evans's Web site: www.towerkill.com.

5. *Elephants:* Find out about the current threats to the survival of African elephants and what you can do to help by contacting

African Wildlife Foundation
1400 16th Street, NW
Suite 120
Washington, DC 20036
www.awf.org

If you have questions about Katy Payne's work with elephants, write to

Elephant Listening Project
159 Sapsucker Woods Road
Ithaca, NY 14850

Her staff would prefer to receive letters rather than e-mail messages or phone calls.

Glossary

bioacoustics—the study of sounds made by living things.

call—a brief sound made by an animal. Often a call is made under certain, identifiable conditions. See *song*.

culling—the selection and removal of certain members of a group. In wildlife biology, culling is the selective killing of individual animals to reduce population size.

echolocation—a technique for locating something by sending out sound, which bounces off of the object or prey, and returns to the listener. Bats use echolocation.

frequency—the highness or lowness of a sound, measured in units called hertz (cycles per second).

geophone—an instrument that measures vibrations passing through soil.

global positioning system (GPS)—a network of satellites that can send signals to a small, handheld receiver to pinpoint the user's position on Earth, in latitude and longitude.

hertz—a unit of frequency (highness or lowness) of a sound, equal to cycles per second.

hydrophone—an underwater microphone.

infrasound—sounds at frequencies under twenty hertz, below the limit of human hearing.

microphone—an instrument that changes sound waves into electronic signals that can be recorded.

pitch—highness or lowness of sound. See *frequency*.

song—a sound of long duration that has identifiable phrases, or groups of notes. In animal songs these phrases are repeated and varied, just like melodies in human songs.

sound—vibrations that travel in waves through air, water, earth, or other materials.

sound spectrogram—a diagram made by a sound spectrograph.

sound spectrograph—a machine that graphs sound, with time on the x axis and frequency on the y axis. A spectrograph helps scientists to compare different kinds of sounds and to see how they vary over time.

PHOTO BY APRIL PULLEY SAYRE

Index